I is for INDIANS of the Southwest

Dedicated to the young seekers and keepers
of all things wild and sacred...

by Judy Rosen & Biff Baird

Judy Rosen began her National Park Service career at Canyon de Chelly National Monument. She has worked as a naturalist and planner in many national parks and forests. She raises two sons while working at Rocky Mountain National Park. Biff Baird earns his living as an interpretive planner, freelance writer, and exhibit designer. A father of two, he prefers hiking, mountain-biking, skiing, and scuba-diving to working.

Illustrations by Rick Wheeler

Rick Wheeler spent several years in northern California where he studied drawing, painting, and illustration at the San Francisco Art Institute and the San Francisco Academy of Art. Influenced by the light and forms of the Colorado Plateau, Rick moved to Moab, Utah in 1995, where he now operates his own award-winning illustration studio.

Front cover: Navajo on horseback at Monument Valley. Inside front cover: Children playing in Canyon de Chelly.
Page 1: Corn, the staff of life for many Southwest Indians, is an important religious symbol.

Edited by Cheri C. Madison. Book design by K. C. DenDooven.

Second Printing, 2001

I IS FOR INDIANS OF THE SOUTHWEST © 2000 KC PUBLICATIONS, INC.
*"The Story Behind the Scenery"; "in pictures... The Continuing Story"; the parallelogram forms
and colors within are registered in the U.S. Patent and Trademark Office.*
LC 00-100134. ISBN 0-88714-211-7.

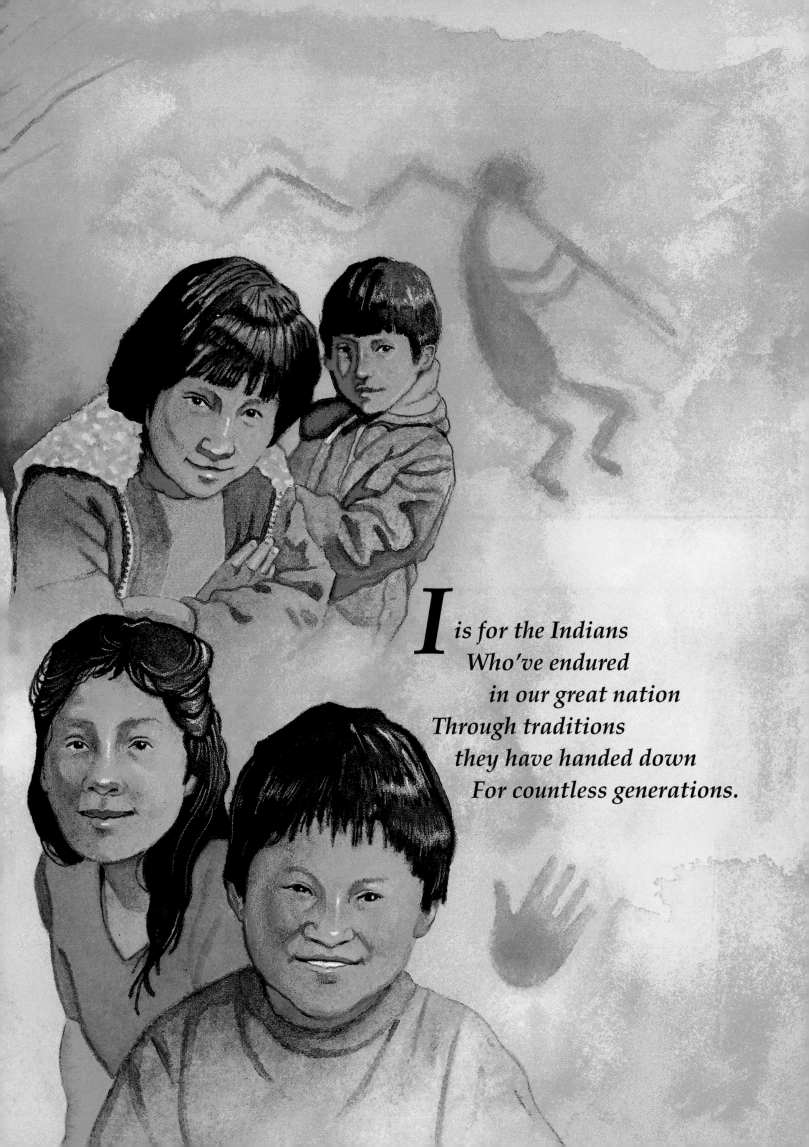

I is for the Indians
  Who've endured
    in our great nation
Through traditions
    they have handed down
      For countless generations.

About Indians of the Southwest

By the time Columbus "discovered" America, people had been living in the Southwest for generations. They descended from roving bands of hunters, who arrived in search of game in the age when great sheets of ice covered the land to the north. These nomads settled, learned to grow corn and other crops, and survived.

The mysterious beauty of the Southwest, from scorching deserts to snowy mountains, shaped these people. It is reflected in their world-famous jewelry, weaving, and pottery, and their traditional way of life.

Navajo, Zuni, Hopi, Apache—these tribes and many more have cultures as diverse as the colors of the rainbow, but they all share an intimacy with nature. When life is a journey through a harsh land, each day is a walk with the spirits of the earth.

Because of corn's importance to Southwest Indian life, corn dances are held in every pueblo to give thanks to the earth and pray for a good harvest.

A is for the **Anasazi**
Who made their homes in cliffs so high.
The Ancient Ones grew squash and corn,
Then disappeared, we don't know why.

A

B is for the **Baskets**
Made from yucca and willow plants,
For storing food and water,
For ceremonies, songs, and dance.

B

C is for the **Cradleboard**,
Baby peeking out,
Safe and snug while watching
What the world is all about.

C

Do you like to dance?

Dances are an important part of Southwest Indian life. They are held to give thanks, celebrate success, cure the sick, and pray for rain. The Navajo *Yei-bi-chei Dance* is part of a healing ceremony that lasts nine days. It is held only in winter, after the snakes are asleep. In the Tewa *animal dance*, small fires are built on rooftops to guide dancers dressed as animals into the village. Animal dances, corn dances, rain dances, and hoop dances . . . all these and more help Southwest Indians find balance and harmony with the natural world.

Deer are honored in Pueblo ceremonies like the Tewa animal dance. They are thanked for the food and clothing they provide.

D is for the **Dances**
To heal the sick and ease their pain,
To keep alive the ancient tales,
To bless the hunt, to bring the rain.

D

E is for the **Eagle Dance**
To praise the bird that soars so high.
It knows the power of the sun,
And flies with spirits in the sky.

E

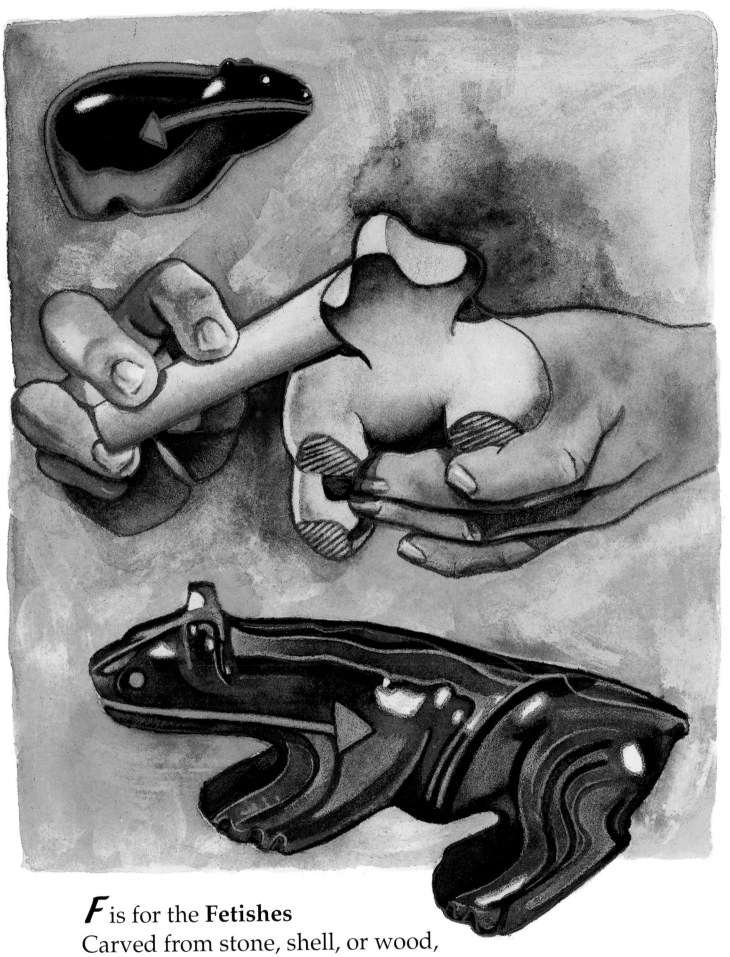

F is for the **Fetishes**
Carved from stone, shell, or wood,
Bringing power to their owners,
Turning bad luck into good.

F

G is for **Geronimo**,
A chief who took a stand.
He led Apache warriors
Against the men who took their land.

G

H is for the **Hopi Tribe**,
Living on the mesas.
Don't you think you'd like to know
What goes on in those places?

H

Indians' Sacred Ways

A Navajo girl sprinkles corn pollen to bless a hogan, and a Corn Dancer offers turkey feathers and evergreen boughs to Corn Mother. A Tohono O'odham elder holds a ripe saguaro fruit over her heart and breathes a silent prayer of thanksgiving. Pueblo hunters offer tobacco, cornmeal, and prayer feathers to animals that have given their lives for food. These sacred ways express reverence for nature and respect for all creatures of the earth.

Southwest Indians believe they are a part of the natural world, not separate from it. Giving thanks to the earth is a way of life in a land that is as harsh as it is beautiful.

I is for the **Indians**
Of the magical Southwest,
Canyons deep and mountains steep,
A land with beauty blessed.

I

Just Jewelry?

Though Southwestern Indian jewelry "dresses up" people all over the world, its earliest use was practical. A concha belt was used to carry silver coins. Or it could be traded for horses, sheep, or goats. Jewelry was also pawned for cash to help a family through lean times, and bought back later.

The Navajo learned to make jewelry from Mexican *plateros*, who traveled the Southwest trading silver trinkets for livestock. Other tribes soon learned the craft and created their own styles.

The earliest jewelry was made from melting or hammering down old silver coins.

Early jewelry was used for trade. What could you trade a silver bracelet or a ring for today?

J is for the **Jewelry**
Of silver, stones, and shells.
Watch the artist while he works.
Learn the story each piece tells.

J

Katsinas for kids!

Katsinas are spirits—of plants, animals, places, and natural forces like wind and rain. There are hundreds of different katsinas.

They are represented in Hopi villages by masked dancers and carved dolls. During ceremonies, dancers bring katsina dolls to Hopi children. The dolls are hung from rafters in their houses, where children learn about the spirits and their powers.

Katsinas help carry prayers to the gods, and teach children about the laws and traditions of their people.

Katsinas are usually friendly, forgiving, and sometimes funny teachers!

K is for **Katsinas**
Carved from roots of cottonwood.
These plant and animal spirits
Teach Hopi children to be good.

K

L is for the **Lands** they live in
Beautiful, but harsh and dry.
Don't you wish that you could paint
The sunset colors in the sky?

L

M is for **Monument Valley**,
Where Navajo herders tend their sheep,
A place you've seen in Western movies,
Sandstone towers, high and steep.

M

Navajo Nation

Long ago the Navajos were hunters who roamed far and wide. They settled in the valleys and canyons of the Southwest around 700 years ago. They learned to farm from the Pueblo people, and how to raise horses and sheep from the Spaniards. Wool from their sheep is woven into beautiful Navajo rugs, for which they are famous.

The traditional Navajo home is the *hogan.* The door of this earth-covered house always faces east to greet the rising sun. Hogans are blessed to make sure they are free of bad spirits.

The Navajo Reservation is bigger than the states of Vermont, New Hampshire, and Connecticut combined.

The Navajo call themselves *Dineh*, "the People," and know their homeland as *Dinetah*, "land of the People."

N is for the **Navajo,**
Largest tribe in the nation.
Parts of three southwestern states
Make up their reservation.

N

Since we may never know
the exact meaning
of pictures left on stone,
let your imagination run wild.
Create your own stories
to go along with
these pictures of the past.

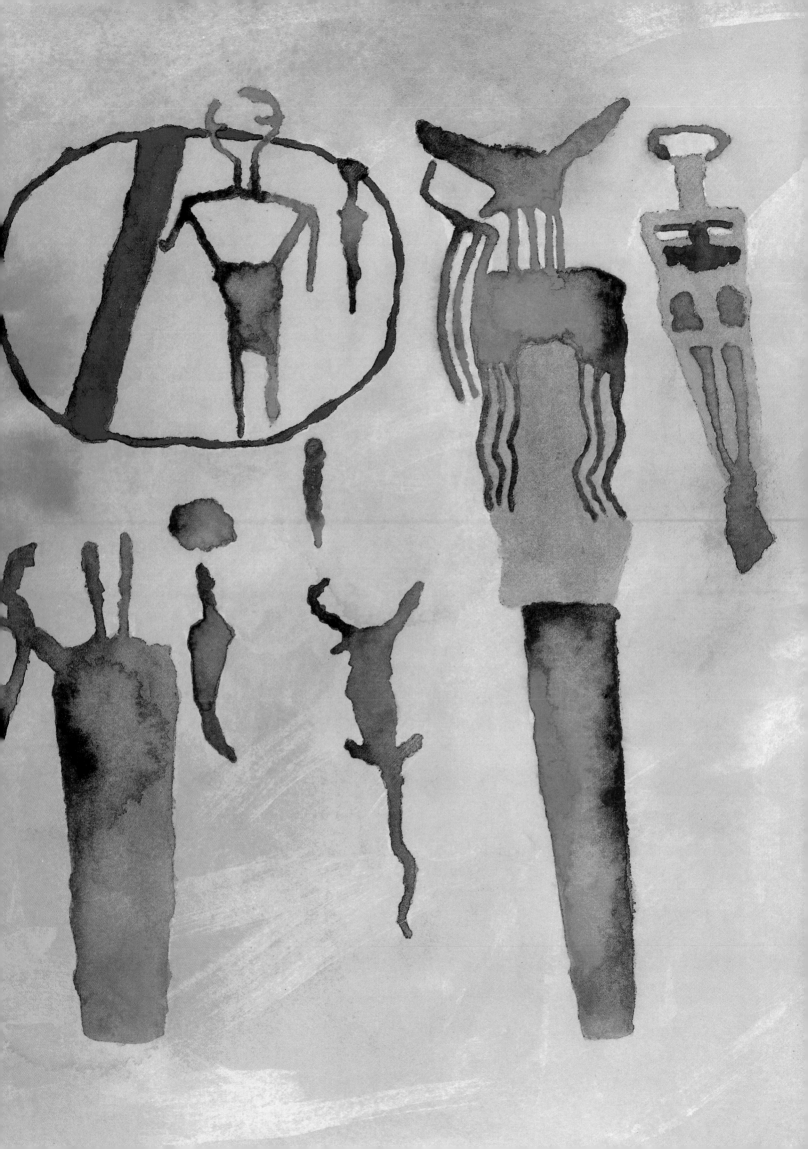

"Once upon a time..."

How were the first people created? Where did they come from? Origin myths are the stories that answer these questions. The Navajo believe that First Man and First Woman were created from an ear of corn. The First People

followed them through four dark worlds beneath the earth. Then they climbed up into this world through a hollow reed.

Some Pueblo tribes also speak of their ancestors moving through a dark underworld in search of light. They finally broke through the crust of the present world with the help of a badger who stood on top of a spruce tree to enlarge a hole made by a woodpecker.

What do *you* believe about how our beautiful world was created?

O is for the **Origin Myths**,
Stories of the world's birth—
How the moon and stars were made,
How people came to walk the earth.

O

P is for **Pottery Shards**,
Puzzle pieces of the past.
If you find some, leave them there
So the stories they tell will last.

P

Q is for the **Quivers** of arrows
Hunters carried on their backs.
Like kids today go to school
With books inside their packs.

Q

Read the rock!

Have you ever wondered what ancient people thought and felt? What their lives were like? Look to the rocks for clues. Early canyon and cliff dwellers of the Southwest left pictures on rock faces. Some were painted. Others were made by chipping away at a big rock with a smaller one. Pictures of deer and bighorn sheep show what they hunted.

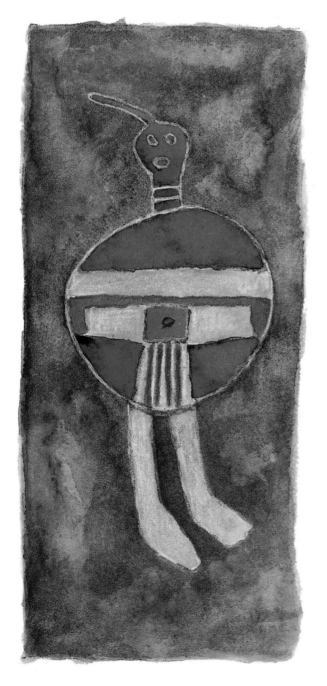

Cornstalks show what they farmed. Some pictures describe their first meetings with white men. Others show details of an entire battle! It was a lot harder to leave messages before there were pens and paper, but the rocks speak to those who listen carefully. Can you hear them?

The country called the United States of America didn't even exist when this pictograph was created. But the artist who painted it used red, white, and blue—the colors of our nation's flag. Do you suppose that is why this pictograph is called the "All-American Man"?

R is for the **Rock Art**,
Ancient language on the stones.
What messages did people leave
Before there were telephones?

R

Sand for sings

The Navajo believe that the universe is held in delicate balance. If this balance is upset, sickness can result. Healing ceremonies, or *sings*, can restore health.

There is a special sandpainting design for each illness. It is created at the sick person's home from colored sand. The patient sits on the sandpainting during the ceremony, receiving prayers, herbs, and chants from the medicine man.

After the sand has absorbed the evil that caused the sickness, it is gathered up and then returned to Mother Earth.

Sandpaintings are also created by modern Navajo artists to be sold as works of art.

S is for **Sandpaintings**,
Made from rocks ground into sand,
For ceremonies to heal the sick
Guided by a medicine man.

S

Taos—one of many tribes

Taos is just one of many Pueblo villages in New Mexico and Arizona. There are hundreds of tribes in the United States. Each pueblo has its own leadership, but they share many traditions and ceremonies.

Among the nation's first farmers, Pueblo people were the first to build permanent homes. Their multi-story houses are the signature of an ancient lifestyle still practiced today.

Many Pueblo people still farm. Others earn a living as potters and jewelers. Some have moved away from the pueblos to find jobs. Those who remain have electricity, glass windows, and pickup trucks parked nearby.

A peek inside a pueblo reveals raised floors and niches used to store pottery.

T is for **Taos Pueblo**,
First apartments in the West.
You'd have to climb a ladder,
If you were a pueblo guest.

T

u is for the bands of **Utes**
In Utah and Colorado,
Gathering plants and hunting deer
In the mountains' shadow.

u

V is for the **Valleys**
Beneath the mountains' snow,
Patches of green between the cliffs,
Where corn and beans can grow.

v

W is for **Weaving**
With wool shorn from the sheep.
Card it, dye it, spin it, weave it
Into treasures you can keep.

W

X is for **San Xavier Mission**,
A place of prayer and celebration.
This "white dove of the desert" is on
The Tohono O'odham Reservation.

X

Yuccas aren't yucky!

Long before there were stores, Southwest Indians relied on nature for their daily needs. The yucca plant was a bargain, providing food, fiber, and soap all in one.

Countless desert plants, even cactus, were used as food, medicine, and dyes. Cholla buds provided protein, and prickly pear cactus fruits were a great source of Vitamin C.

Sage was used to heal wounds or brewed into tea to ease cramps. The juniper tree had many uses, too.

Its soft bark once lined cradleboards. Its berries were crushed into insect repellent. Its seeds still are strung as necklaces.

Navajo rugs reflect the warm hues of the plants used to dye the wool of the sheep.

Next time you are out in nature, look at the grocery store all around you.

Cure for the Common Cold

1 tiny branch of juniper
1 tiny branch of pinyon
pinyon pitch
dash of sage

Harp on it to soften it all up.
Boil it all up. Sit under a blanket
with this over a boiling fire.
Inhale like a vapor and sweat.

Y is for the **Yucca** plant,
Its roots made into soap.
Its leaves were finely woven
Into baskets, sandals, and rope.

Y

Zuni ways

The Zuni stand out among the Pueblo tribes for their skills at fetish carving and working with stone, shell, and silver. Like most Pueblo tribes, they still follow old traditions.

One of these is holding the *Shalako*—an annual house-blessing ceremony. Dancers dress up as huge bird-like figures, called *shalakos*, who are messengers of the rainmakers. They also re-enact ancient Zuni legends. Held in early winter, the ceremony lasts 49 days!

Next time you celebrate Thanksgiving, Hanukkah, or Christmas, think of Zunis holding the *Shalako*, a spectacular ceremony uniquely their own.

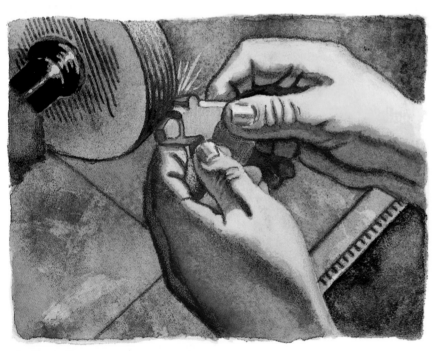

A fetish may take the shape of a mountain lion, bobcat, bear, coyote, shrew, or ear of corn. It may be decorated with beads and feathers, or bundled in buckskin. It may even include a live toad!

Z is for the **Zuni**.
Craftwork is their pride.
For jewelry and fetishes
They are famous far and wide.

Z

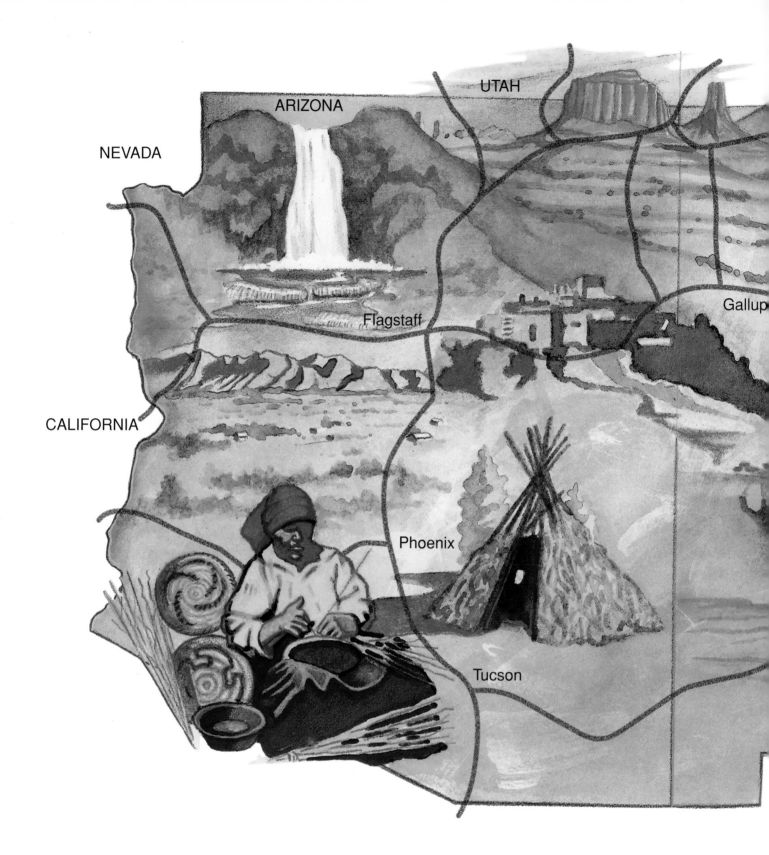

NEVADA

ARIZONA

UTAH

Gallup

Flagstaff

CALIFORNIA

Phoenix

Tucson

Top Three Adventures in Indian Country

❶ Visit a cliff dwelling. Take a ranger-led tour through Cliff Palace at Mesa Verde National Park, or hike down to White House Ruin in Canyon de Chelly National Monument.

❷ Attend a Pueblo dance. Some ceremonies are open to the public, but times and places vary throughout the Pueblo villages. Inquire locally or log on to www.indianpueblo.org/pueblo.calendar.html.

COLORADO
NEW MEXICO

Santa Fe

TEXAS

Indian Country

When Christopher Columbus sailed from Spain in 1492, he was looking for India. He landed on an island in the Caribbean Sea instead. Thinking he had reached India, he called the inhabitants *Indians*. Despite the fact that Columbus was halfway around the world from where he hoped he was, the name stuck. Many Indians today prefer to be called *Native Americans* or *First Americans*, both of which are more accurate than *Indians*.

There are over 300 tribes in the United States. The nearly 40 tribes in the Southwest live in Arizona, New Mexico, Utah, and Colorado. Where these four states touch, many cultures come together.

Indian Reservations of the Southwest

❸ Look for rock art. Read Newspaper Rock, filled with petroglyphs, in Petrified Forest National Park, or discover larger-than-life pictographs at the Great Gallery in Canyonlands National Park.

What do you mean by . . . ?

Anasazi—ancestors of the Pueblo people who lived in canyons and on mesa tops in the Southwest from approximately A.D. 200 to A.D. 1450

cliff dwellers—name given to the Anasazi because of their custom of building homes in cliffs and rock overhangs

fetish—an object believed to have magical powers

hogan—the earth-covered traditional Navajo home

katsina—Pueblo spirit beings that can grant good luck and carry prayers to the gods

kiva—a circular room used by the Pueblo people for rituals

maize—corn, a grain native to the New World

mesa—a land formation with a flat top and steep sides

niche—a recess in a wall used for holding and storing things

nomads—people who move from place to place according to the food supply

origin myth—stories and beliefs about how the first people came to be

petroglyphs—pictures or symbols chiseled into rock

pictographs—pictures or symbols painted on rock

plateros—Mexican silversmiths who roamed the Southwest trading silver trinkets for livestock

pueblo—Spanish word for village, referring to Southwest Indians who built impressive stone and adobe dwellings

shard—piece or fragment of ancient pottery

sing—a Navajo healing ceremony that includes songs, chants, prayers, and herbs

Tohono O'odham—formerly known as the Papago, the "desert people" who live in the Sonoran Desert of southern Arizona and northern Mexico

Did you know that . . .?

. . .During World War II, the Navajo developed a code in their own language that the enemies were never able to break. This helped the United States to win the war.

. . .Trading posts were the first contact points between Southwest Indians and the United States government. They served as banks, post offices, and stores.

. . .One pound of pinyon pine nuts equals 3,000 calories—good news if you had to survive in the high deserts before grocery stores. That's more than three huge banana splits!

More books you'll enjoy!

For Kids

The Apaches and Navajos, by CRAIG A. and KATHERINE M. DOHERTY. Franklin Watts.

Coyote and Little Turtle: A Traditional Hopi Tale, by HERSCHEL TALASHOEMA, edited by EMORY SEKAQUAPTEWA. Clear Light Publishing.

Coyote Stories of the Navajo People, edited by ROBERT ROESSEL, JR. and DILLON PLATERO. Navajo Curriculum Press.

Giving Thanks, A Native American Good Morning Message, by CHIEF JAKE SWAMP. Lee & Low Books, Inc.

The Hopis, A First Americans Book, by VIRGINIA DRIVING HAWK SNEVE. Holiday House.

I'm in Charge of Celebrations, by BYRD BAYLOR. Charles Scribner's Sons.

The Navajos, A First Americans Book, by VIRGINIA DRIVING HAWK SNEVE. Holiday House.

Navajo: Visions and Voices Across the Mesa, by SHONTO BEGAY. Scholastic Press.

The Old Hogan, by MARGARET KAHN GARAWAY. Old Hogan Publishing.

The People Shall Continue, by SIMON J. ORTIZ. Children's Book Press.

From KC Publications

Southwestern Indian Arts & Crafts, by TOM BAHTI and MARK BAHTI.

Southwestern Indian Tribes, by TOM BAHTI and MARK BAHTI.

Southwestern Indian Ceremonials, by TOM BAHTI and MARK BAHTI.

Southwestern Indian Pottery, by BRUCE HUCKO.

Southwestern Indian Weaving, by MARK BAHTI.

Zuni Fetishes, by FRANK HAMILTON CUSHING. Expanded Version by MARK BAHTI.

Monument Valley: The Story Behind the Scenery, by K. C. DENDOOVEN.

Canyon de Chelly: The Story Behind the Scenery, by CHARLES SUPPLEE and DOUGLAS and BARBARA ANDERSON.

in pictures...Canyon de Chelly: The Continuing Story, by WILSON HUNTER, JR.

Mesa Verde: The Story Behind the Scenery, by LINDA MARTIN.

The Navajo Treaty—1868.

What Does the Future Hold?

For thousands of years, people have made a living in the dry rugged lands of the Southwest. Long before there were supermarkets or electricity, they hunted, farmed, and gathered wild plants, ever-mindful of the earth that sustained them. Their way of life and knowledge of the earth have been passed down from generation to generation.

Will these traditions survive the 21st century? When the keepers of the sacred knowledge pass on, will their wisdom die with them? Today's Southwest Indians walk with one foot in the old world and one in the new. We would do well to learn about their ancient way of looking at the world, of trying to live in harmony with nature rather than trying to control it. For all our computers and rocket ships, we may need that knowledge now more than ever.

KC Publications has been the leading publisher of colorful, interpretive books about National Park areas, public lands, Indian lands, and related subjects for over 37 years. We have 6 active series—over 125 titles—with Translation Packages in up to 8 languages for over half the areas we cover. Write, call, or visit our web site for our full-color catalog.

Our series are:

The Story Behind the Scenery® – Compelling stories of over 65 National Park areas and similar Public Land areas. Some with Translation Packages.

*in pictures... **The Continuing Story**® – A companion, pictorially oriented, series on America's National Parks. All titles have Translation Packages.

For Young Adventurers™ – Dedicated to young seekers and keepers of all things wild and sacred. Explore America's Heritage from A to Z.

Voyage of Discovery™ – Exploration of the expansion of the western United States.

Indian Culture and the Southwest – All about Native Americans, past and present.

Calendars – For National Parks and Southwest Indian culture, in dramatic full color, and a companion Color Your Own series, with crayons.

To receive our full-color catalog featuring over 125 titles—Books, Calendars, Screen Scenes, Videos, Audio Tapes, and other related specialty products:

Call (800-626-9673), fax (702-433-3420), write to the address below, Or visit our web site at www.kcpublications.com

Published by KC Publications, 3245 E. Patrick Ln., Suite A, Las Vegas, NV 89120.

Inside back cover:
Throughout the ages, people have found ways to say, "I was here!"

Back cover:
Tradition in motion.

Created, Designed, and Published in the U.S.A.
Printed by Tien Wah Press (Pte.) Ltd, Singapore